The Sozo Life

The Sozo Life

How One Question from God Led to My Greatest Discovery

Johnny Jones

Copyright © 2022 John E Jones
ISBN: 979-8-9863558-0-1

Scripture taken from the New King James Version®. Copyright © 1982 by Thomas Nelson. Used by permission. All rights reserved.

Scripture taken from the Amplified Bible, Copyright © 1954, 1958, 1962, 1964, 1965, 1987 by The Lockman Foundation. Used by permission.

Scripture quotations marked CSB have been taken from the Christian Standard Bible®, Copyright © 2017 by Holman Bible Publishers. Used by permission. Christian Standard Bible® and CSB® are federally registered trademarks of Holman Bible Publishers.

Scripture quotations from The Authorized (King James) Version. Rights in the Authorized Version in the United Kingdom are vested in the Crown. Reproduced by permission of the Crown's patentee, Cambridge University Press

Scriptures taken from the Holy Bible, New International Version®, NIV®. Copyright © 1973, 1978, 1984, 2011 by Biblica, Inc.™ Used by permission of Zondervan. All rights reserved worldwide. www.zondervan.com The "NIV" and "New International Version" are trademarks registered in the United States Patent and Trademark Office by Biblica, Inc.®

Scripture quotations marked (NLT) are taken from the Holy Bible, New Living Translation, copyright ©1996, 2004, 2015 by Tyndale House Foundation. Used by permission of Tyndale House Publishers, Carol Stream, Illinois 60188. All rights reserved.

Cover design by Day One Creative

Table of Contents

TABLE OF CONTENTS III

INTRODUCTION V

CHAPTER ONE 1

CHAPTER TWO: *SAVED* 9

CHAPTER THREE: *HEALED* 27

CHAPTER FOUR: *DELIVERED* 37

CHAPTER FIVE: *PRESERVED* 45

CHAPTER SIX: *PROTECTED* 51

CHAPTER SEVEN: *MAKE PROSPEROUS* 59

CHAPTER EIGHT: *MAKE WHOLE* 70

CHAPTER NINE: TASTE AND SEE 78

CHAPTER TEN: HOW TO RECEIVE 88

CHAPTER ELEVEN: YOUR SOZO STORY 103

CHAPTER TWELVE: *TAKE YOUR SEAT* 119

ACKNOWLEDGMENTS 125

Introduction

You may have heard the story of Charles Spurgeon's visit with a parishioner in his church, a poor elderly lady in her final days.

As the story goes, while chatting with her, Spurgeon began to look around the room of her dilapidated home when something caught his eye. It was an old, yellowed framed document that had no doubt been sitting on her wall for decades. With deep curiosity, Spurgeon asked the frail lady if she knew what it was, to which she replied that she wasn't quite sure.

She went on to explain that she had worked as a caregiver for a wealthy estate owner for many years and that at his passing she was given this beautiful document, which she framed and placed on her wall.

Spurgeon then proceeded to inform her that this "beautiful document" was actually the deed to the man's estate and that all the while, as she was living in abject poverty, she could have enjoyed so much more.

Sadly, for many of us, our lot has been similar to this lady's. Jesus died and rose again to give us so much more than most of us have ever known.

For whatever reason, through either religious tradition or incomplete teaching, our adversary has kept us from experiencing and walking in all that Jesus came to give us.

> *Our adversary has kept us from experiencing and walking in all that Jesus came to give us.*

My prayer is that as you read this book with an open heart and mind, the Holy Spirit will help you discover your full inheritance through the finished work of Jesus on the cross. Many have settled for living a so-so Christian life, but our heavenly Father wants so much more for us than that. Being the good, good Father that He is, He desires that we live and enjoy the Sozo Life.

Chapter One:
The Question

It's impossible to remember every moment in life, but there are some moments that can't be forgotten. One such moment happened for me in the summer of 2000.

I had just attended a Christian leadership conference in Oklahoma. The conference had just wrapped up that morning and I was enjoying a nice lunch at an Italian restaurant right across the street from the conference arena. My friend Bruce sat right across from me. It was our second year attending the conference together. Knowing that I would be speaking at the church I pastored that coming Sunday, Bruce asked me what I was going to speak on. "I'm sure you've got a notebook full of notes," he said.

I didn't have a notebook full of notes because I've never really been much of a note taker. I've found that while I'm busy taking notes on the last thing I heard, I'm missing the thing that's being said in the moment.

So, I try to absorb as much as I can and then go back and listen to the audio. My response to Bruce's question was, "I'm not sure what I'm going to speak on."

Right then and there I heard another question, but this one wasn't from Bruce. At first, I wasn't quite sure where it came from, but I heard it loud and clear. "Do you know how saved you really are?"

> *"Do you know how saved you really are?"*

At first, I thought this question was some random thought that had hit my mind, but it wouldn't go away. I continued to hear it over and over for the next several days. When the question in my head continued into the next week, I was pretty sure it had to be from the Lord. And I knew that in this question, the Lord was trying to bring me to a discovery.

At that point in my life, if you had asked me what it meant to be saved, I would have given you the typical answer. Growing up in church my whole life, my answer to this question would have been the same as everyone else around me. I would have said that to be saved means that you have trusted Jesus as your Savior and received forgiveness for your sins through His death on the cross.

This means your name is written in the Lamb's Book of Life and when you die, you'll spend eternity in Heaven with the Lord and all the saints and loved ones who have gone on before.

My Greatest Discovery

To be honest, looking up a word that I felt I already knew the meaning of seemed foolish. But pushing that feeling aside, I grabbed my Strong's Exhaustive Concordance and looked up the meaning of the word saved. Since the Old Testament was written in Hebrew and the New Testament in Greek, to really understand the full meaning of any word or phrase in Scripture, you must look it up in the original language in which it was written.

The verse that came to mind to look up, which would allow me to do a word study on the word saved, was John 3:17. Parked right beside John 3:17 is perhaps the most famous verse in the Bible. Most kids in church can quote John 3:16: "For God so loved the world that He gave His only begotten Son, that whoever believes in Him should not perish but have everlasting life." John 3:17 goes on to say, "For God did not send His Son into the world to condemn the world, but that the world through Him might be saved."

It was when I looked up the word saved that I, for the very first time, saw the Greek word sozo. I began to look up saved everywhere I could find it in the New Testament, and sure enough I saw the word sozo every time! With my legal pad beside me, I began to write down all the definitions for saved/sozo I was able to determine from each of its mentions in the New Testament. There were seven definitions

> *There were seven definitions I wrote down: "to be saved, healed, delivered, preserved, protected, made prosperous, and made whole."*

I wrote down: "to be saved, healed, delivered, preserved, protected, made prosperous, and made whole." I was absolutely shocked, to say the least, and thought, Surely this can't be the meaning of the word saved everywhere you see it in the New Testament.

The word saved is used no less than 110 times in the New Testament, and in every case, it is translated from the Greek word sozo. In fact, Jesus used the word sozo interchangeably, as we see in the story of the woman with the issue of blood. Luke 8:48 says, "And he said unto her, Daughter, be of good comfort: thy faith hath made thee whole; go in peace" (KJV). The word "whole" in this verse is the Greek word sozo. So why didn't Jesus just tell her that her faith had healed her? Because this lady had more than one need. Mark 5:26 tells us that she "had suffered many things from many physicians. She had spent all that she had and was no better, but rather grew worse."

> *Jesus didn't just want to heal her that day; He wanted to make her completely whole. And that's exactly what He wants for you and me.*

Not only had this lady been sick for twelve years, but in her effort to find a cure, she found herself completely bankrupt. You see, Jesus didn't just want to heal her that day; He wanted to make her completely whole. And that's exactly what He wants for you and me. Second Peter 1:3 says, "According as his divine power hath given unto us all things that pertain unto life and godliness, through the knowledge of him that hath called us to glory and virtue" (KJV). Through the power of His complete and finished work on the cross, Jesus has provided everything we need for life and godliness. These words "life and godliness" are defined as "the God kind of life," or "abundant life."

Jesus said in John 10:10, "The thief does not come except to steal, and to kill, and to destroy. I have come that they may have life, and that they may have it more abundantly." This same verse in the Amplified Bible says, "The thief comes only in order to steal and kill and destroy. I came that they may have life and enjoy life, and have it in abundance [to the full, till it overflows].

Most Christians today are not enjoying the abundant life that Jesus came to give us. There is no real excitement about their salvation. Yes, we're glad to know that when we die, we'll go to heaven, but that day seems so far off. What most believers have yet to discover is that the Gospel (Good News) is as much for the Christian as it is for the unsaved. Today is the day of salvation. The

> *The Good News of what Jesus has done for us is as much for the believer today as it is for the sinner!*

Good News of what Jesus has done for us is as much for the believer today as it is for the sinner! The apostle Paul said in 2 Corinthians 2:15 that we "are being saved," which speaks to the ongoing process of salvation as much as it does the one-time event.

Yes, you were saved when you asked Jesus into your life and received Him as your Savior, but this salvation (sozo) is also for every day and every area of your life. Is there anything that needs saving in your life today? Does your marriage need saving? Does your health need saving? Are there relationships in your life that need saving? Whatever needs saving, Jesus is the answer! The name of Jesus defined means "Jehovah is Salvation."

Chapter One Study Guide Questions

Do you remember a time or moment in your life when the Lord asked you a question that led to a divine discovery? If so, list the question and discovery.

_____
_____
_____

Prior to reading this chapter, how would you have described or defined being saved?

_____
_____
_____

Using a Greek concordance, or BlueLetterBible.org, look up the word saved in John 3:17 and the word salvation in Romans 1:16. Write down every definition that you find for the words saved and salvation. Note: Step-by-step directions for using blueletterbible.org are included at the end of the book.

_____
_____
_____

What has this chapter helped you discover about being saved?

_____
_____

Chapter Two:

Saved

Let's look at each one of the seven definitions of the word saved/sozo, starting with the first, and what may be the most important.

Think about this for a moment. If you were drowning in a river and someone threw you a life ring and pulled you back to shore, they would be saving you from drowning and death. At the same time, they would also be saving you to something — the shore, and the rest of your life.

In that moment in the river your first thought would most likely be that you didn't want to drown and die, but once you were pulled to the safety of the shore you would be able to think about living.

You see, most of us get saved because we don't want to die and go to hell, which is a very good reason!

> *It is impossible to be saved from something without simultaneously being saved to something.*

But at the same time, it is impossible to be saved from something without simultaneously being saved to something. If you understand this foundational truth, then it makes it easy to understand all the aspects and benefits of sozo. Even in the first and foundational part of sozo, which is being saved, we are saved both from and to. We are saved from separation from God and saved to righteousness or being made right with God. This one truth is the mother of all understanding when it comes to being saved/sozo. And to really understand the truth of being saved, we must start all the way back at the beginning with Adam and Eve in the Garden of Eden.

In the Garden Adam and Eve had everything they could ever want or need. The Father had given them His full supply and on top of that they enjoyed unhindered fellowship with Him. They woke up every morning in right standing with God and nothing stood between them and the Father. All of that ended, however, when Satan disguised himself as a serpent and deceived Eve through a lie that started as a question: "Did God really tell you?" His question to Eve led her to doubt God's word, then Satan convinced her that God was trying to withhold all-knowing wisdom and knowledge from her. She bought the lie, ate the fruit, then offered it to her husband, to which he partook. They were then banned from the Garden, losing everything they had known, most

> *God was letting the devil know that there was a Seed that would be coming to right this wrong and bring about the restoration of all that was lost.*

importantly their status of being right with God. Sin had brought about a separation that they could not repair. All hope was not lost, however, as God gave hope in His own words when He pronounced judgment upon Satan and Adam and Eve. Notice what God said to them in Genesis 3:15: "And I will put enmity between you and the woman, and between your seed and her Seed; He shall bruise your head, and you shall bruise His heel." Do you notice the capitalized "S" in the word "Seed"? The earliest translators of the original manuscripts knew that this "Seed" was speaking of someone of divine origin. And we have the benefit of knowing that this "Seed" is Jesus Christ.

God was letting the devil know that there was a Seed that would be coming to right this wrong and bring about the restoration of all that was lost. God was letting the devil and future mankind know that although Satan may bruise His heel, resulting in a temporary injury, this Seed would bring the devil a death blow. However, to bring this about God would need a way in. Which begs the question, "If God is God why couldn't He have just come down from Heaven and fixed the whole mess in an instant?" The answer is because our God is a God of order.

In Genesis 1:28-31 God gave complete authority over the earth to Adam and Eve and He couldn't just violate His own order by illegally righting a wrong. To restore back man's God-given authority God would need to do so in a legal manner, and the legal way would be through covenant.

The Devil Don't Know Everything

As an interesting side note, it's easy to see that although the devil may be smart, he is certainly not omniscient like our heavenly Father. In fact, every time the devil thought God was raising up the "Seed" that would bring about his demise, he would attempt to destroy, or at least disqualify, that person.

We see this with Adam and Eve's first two sons, Cain and Abel. Satan thought that because Abel's offering was accepted and Cain's was rejected that Abel must be the "Seed," so he murdered Abel through his brother Cain.

We continue to see this through Moses when Pharaoh issued a decree for all the Hebrew baby boys to be killed. In the Gospels we see that even Herod, upon learning that the Messiah had been born in Bethlehem, issued the order for all the baby boys there to be put to death as well. Even when Jesus was about to begin His ministry and it had been made known to all that He was the Son of God, the devil attempted to disqualify Jesus in the forty days of testing in the wilderness.

A Covenant Thing

The first message I ever shared as a pastor was on Easter Sunday at what was the launch of a new

> *"Easter, A Covenant Thing."*

church plant where I lived in Raleigh, North Carolina. I was nervous to say the least and relying on the Lord to give me a word for His people for that special day. What He gave me blew me away, and to my surprise I had never heard it before. I titled the message that day "Easter, A Covenant Thing." What the Lord showed me was that Resurrection Sunday was all made possible through a covenant and that covenant went all the way back to Abraham.

Even as a child whenever I heard the story of Abraham offering Isaac it never quite set well with me. I couldn't get my mind around the fact that God would do that to a father who had waited so long for a son. Though I would never say it, in my mind I thought, what a cruel way to test a man's love, by asking him to sacrifice his only son!

What the Lord showed me was that this was not about testing Abraham for the sake of testing him, but rather it was God looking for a legal way to get Jesus into the earth. That legal way was through the covenant God and Abraham had established. Abraham didn't understand all of this, but he was willing to sacrifice his son for the Lord. And because Isaac was the promised son, Abraham knew that God would have to restore him, based on God's own word. Up until that time in history there was no record of anyone being raised from the dead, yet Abraham believed that God would have to raise his son Isaac from the dead if he sacrificed him. Hebrews 11:19 says, "Abraham reasoned that God could even raise the dead, and so in a manner of speaking he did receive Isaac back from death" (NIV). We even see this in what Abraham said to his servants before he went up that mountain in Genesis 22:5. He said, "Stay here with the donkey while I and the boy go over there. We will worship and then we will come back to you" (NIV).

So, what exactly was this whole thing about? God was looking for a legal way into the earth to right the wrong that had happened back in the Garden of Eden, and He found that legal way through Abraham.

> *God was looking for a legal way into the earth to right the wrong that had happened back in the Garden of Eden, and He found that legal way through Abraham.*

God wasn't just testing Abraham; He was testing the covenant between them.

If you understand the guides of covenant, then you understand that when one party in covenant gives their best to the other, the receiver must reciprocate with their best. This is great when you're in covenant with someone greater than you in status or wealth. If I'm in covenant with someone much wealthier than me, for example, and I give them my best watch, a Timex, then they must reciprocate with their best watch, which might be a Rolex. When Abraham gave his only son whom he loved to God, it allowed God in a legal way to give His only Son whom He loved, and God's Son, Jesus, is a much better Son.

I'm not sure that Abraham even realized how prophetic his answer to Isaac was when Isaac him asked about the sacrifice. As they were headed up the mountain, Isaac said, "Dad, I see the wood, the fire, and the knife, but where's the sacrifice?" According to Genesis 22:8 Abraham responded by saying, "My son, God will provide himself a lamb for a burnt offering: so they went both of them together" (KJV). Yes, God did indeed provide a Lamb, "the Lamb of God who takes away the sin of the world!" (John 1:29).

Righteousness By Faith

So, what exactly made Abraham the "standout" person God could have such a powerful covenant with? It was all about "righteousness by faith." Simply put, according to Genesis 15:6 Abraham "believed in the Lord, and He accounted it to him for righteousness."

The Lord knew that despite man's best effort, we would never, in and through our own ability, be able to be right with God, or righteous. God knew that when the "Seed" would come one day that we would have to put our faith and trust in the "Seed," Jesus, to be made right with God. So, He chose Abraham because he was the first to receive righteousness by faith. Let's be honest, Abraham wasn't perfect. He was far from it. Abraham was born a sinner just like all of us and it showed up from time to time in his life. Twice he lied about his wife being his sister, and who knows what else he may have done throughout his long life.

What made Abraham "right with God" and qualified him to have such an amazing covenant with God was his simple belief. He was the first one to "believe God" and thus is known as the "father of us all," according to Romans 4:16. Paul explained this in Romans 3:21-26:

> But now apart from the law the righteousness of God has been made known, to which the Law and the Prophets testify. This righteousness is given through faith in Jesus Christ to all who believe. There is no difference between Jew and Gentile, for all have sinned and fall short of the glory of God, and all are

justified freely by his grace through the redemption that came by Christ Jesus. God presented Christ as a sacrifice of atonement, through the shedding of his blood—to be received by faith. He did this to demonstrate his righteousness, because in his forbearance he had left the sins committed beforehand unpunished—he did it to demonstrate his righteousness at the present time, so as to be just and the one who justifies those who have faith in Jesus (NIV).

Jesus, the "Second Adam," made everything right between us and the Father, giving us right standing with God. Second Corinthians 5:21 says, "For God made Christ, who never sinned, to be the offering for our sin, so that we could be made right with God through Christ" (NLT).

> *Jesus, the "Second Adam," made everything right between us and the Father, giving us right standing with God.*

So why is this truth about "righteousness by faith" so important for us to understand? And what makes it foundational to walking in the Sozo Life? It's only when we understand that everything has been made right between us and the Father, that we are able to receive all that He has done for us and given to us through Jesus. The first part of sozo, saved, is so important to understand because we see that in God giving Jesus to make us right with Him, He saved us from eternal damnation and then saved us to abundant life. Understanding this truth also makes it much easier to receive everything else the Father provided for us through Jesus. Romans 8:32 says, "He who did not spare his own Son, but gave him up for us all — how will he not also, along with him, graciously give us all things?" (NIV).

The Power of Knowing

There is a foundational power that comes from knowing our sins are forgiven and that we have been made right with God. Knowing this truth sets us up to receive whatever is lacking in our lives. Let's look at a story that so beautifully illustrates this. In Luke 5:17-26 we read:

> One day Jesus was teaching, and Pharisees and teachers of the law were sitting there. They had come

from every village of Galilee and from Judea and Jerusalem. And the power of the Lord was with Jesus to heal the sick. Some men came carrying a paralyzed man on a mat and tried to take him into the house to lay him before Jesus. When they could not find a way to do this because of the crowd, they went up on the roof and lowered him on his mat through the tiles into the middle of the crowd, right in front of Jesus.

When Jesus saw their faith, he said, "Friend, your sins are forgiven." The Pharisees and the teachers of the law began thinking to themselves, "Who is this fellow who speaks blasphemy? Who can forgive sins but God alone?"

Jesus knew what they were thinking and asked, "Why are you thinking these things in your hearts? Which is easier: to say, 'Your sins are forgiven,' or to say, 'Get up and walk'? But I want you to know that the Son of Man has authority on earth to forgive sins."

So, he said to the paralyzed man, "I tell you, get up, take your mat and go home."

Immediately he stood up in front of them, took what he had been lying on and went home praising God. Everyone was amazed and gave praise to God. They were filled with awe and said, "We have seen remarkable things today."

Jesus knew that for this man to receive the healing he needed, he would have to know his sins had been forgiven. Do you know that your sins have been forgiven?

Do you also know that you have been made right with God and that because of what Jesus did for you on the cross nothing stands in the way between you and the Father?

You may be thinking, "Yes, Johnny, but I still mess up, and in those moments, I don't feel very righteous." I get it. Sin doesn't make us feel very righteous, and that's why our adversary is constantly trying to pull us into sin. But here's the truth: You're not a sinner because you sin. You're a sinner because you were born a

> *You're made righteous through being born again, or the second birth.*

sinner. And in the same way you're not righteous because you do righteous stuff.

You're made righteous through being born again, or the second birth.

As the first Adam made us sinners, the Second Adam, Jesus Christ, makes us righteous. As a born-again child of God, righteousness isn't what you do, but who you are. Second Corinthians 5:21 tells us that we've been made the righteousness of God through Christ Jesus. If you've never received this free gift of righteousness given to us through Christ, would you receive it right now by faith? Paul explained how simple it is to receive it in Romans 10:8-12:

"The message is very close at hand; it is on your lips and in your heart."

And that message is the very message about faith that we preach: If you openly declare that Jesus is Lord and believe in your heart that God raised him from the dead, you will be saved. For it is by believing in your heart that you are made right with God, and it is by openly declaring your faith that you are saved. As the

Scriptures tell us, "Anyone who trusts in him will never be disgraced." Jew and Gentile are the same in this respect. They have the same Lord, who gives generously to all who call on him (NLT).

Right now, right where you are, pray a simple prayer like this straight from your heart to the Father:

Heavenly Father, I come to You right now, the best I know how, by faith. I declare with my mouth and from my heart that I believe Jesus Christ is Your Son. That He came to this earth to be the Lamb of God that would take away my sin. I confess Jesus as my Lord and Savior. By faith I receive the forgiveness of sin and the gift of righteousness. Thank You for making me right with You, Father, and thank You for all that this salvation brings into my life. In Jesus' name, Amen!

> *If you prayed that prayer from your heart, with your mouth by faith, then let me be the first to say, "Welcome to the family of God!"*

If you prayed that prayer from your heart, with your mouth by faith, then let me be the first to say, "Welcome to the family of God!" I'm so happy for you, more so than words can even describe. Let someone know what has happened in your life, and at your first opportunity go public with your faith through believer's baptism. You have now embarked on a lifelong journey with the Lord. Now, let's discover six of the other things your salvation package includes.

Chapter Two Study Guide Questions

Below, write down some things that Jesus has saved you to. Then list things that Jesus has saved you from.

_____

_____

_____

As a believer in Jesus Christ, how does the truth that you have been made right with God impact your life?

_____

_____

_____

Righteousness is not based on what we do, but rather based on who we now are as believers. How does this truth impact your daily life?

_____

_____

_____

How does knowing that salvation is based upon a covenant God made with Jesus and ratified through Christ's finished work on the cross impact your ability to receive salvation? Is it something you must continually work for, or can you rest in the work of another?

_____

_____

Chapter Three:
Healed

My friend Mike was thirty-five and on staff with a large church in Hawaii. He loved his job and he loved people, especially young people. Mike had a heart for young boys who had no father figure in their lives. Often out of his own pocket Mike would take a group of boys out to eat, or get Jamba Juice, a Hawaiian favorite, and have Bible study with them to disciple them. He saw the fruit of this labor as many of these young boys gave their hearts and lives to Christ.

On one such Friday night outing Mike took the boys skating, and while they were waiting in line to get in one of the boys, sitting on a railing near Mike, slipped. Mike reached out to soften the fall, but the boy's hand came sharply and forcefully down on Mike's neck. Mike felt as if something had happened in his neck but had no idea as to the severity.

The next day Mike gathered the boys together to go to a boxcar racing venue. Just as they arrived, Mike began to feel weak and disoriented. Suddenly he began to lose any sensation on the right side of his body and couldn't walk and had a hard time speaking.

The boys were all scared and worried for Mike. One of the boys called his mom, who happened to be a nurse. She told her son to get Mike in the car and rush him to the hospital. The oldest of the boys was only fifteen and had no driver's license, yet they did as told and rushed Mike to the ER. That mom had called ahead to the hospital, so medical staff were standing by to treat Mike. The doctors immediately began to put Mike through a series of tests and an extensive CT scan. The scans revealed that the main artery in Mike's neck had been torn from the accidental blow he had received the previous night. A blood clot had formed in the artery and had somehow worked itself loose and made its way to the brain, thus causing Mike to have a severe stroke.

Word began to spread quickly about Mike's condition, and soon many believers were praying for him. The boys all gathered in the waiting area and prayed earnestly for their friend and mentor to be healed. Pastor Wayne, senior pastor of the church where

Mike was on staff, told the church about Mike's condition right there in the Saturday night service and led the whole congregation in a powerful prayer of healing for Mike.

Over the next few days Mike began to quickly improve, much to the amazement of the medical staff, so the lead physician treating Mike ordered a new CT scan. The original CT scan had clearly shown the tear in Mike's artery, but the new scan painted a different picture. Through the power of prayer and the healing that came along with Mike's salvation package, sozo, there was absolutely no sign or trace of any tear in Mike's artery. He continued to defy all medical norms as he walked out his complete and total healing.

Healing Is Included in the Package

Did you notice above where I wrote the words "Mike's salvation package"? That's exactly what healing is. Healing is one of the seven components, or benefits, to being saved and made possible by the finished work of Jesus on the cross. Looking ahead at the cross, Isaiah prophetically wrote in Isaiah 53:5, "by his wounds we are healed" (NIV). Peter, looking back at the cross, said in 1 Peter 2:24, "for by His wounds you [who believe] have been healed" (AMP). David wrote in Psalm 68:19 "Blessed be the Lord, who daily loads us with benefits, the God of our salvation! Selah." "Selah" in Hebrew means "to think about it" or "to think on it."

Think for a moment about just how good our heavenly Father is to provide healing for us through His Son Jesus Christ.

Healing is just as much your right to receive by faith, because of what Jesus did for you, as being saved from hell and given eternal life!

> *Healing is just as much your right to receive by faith, because of what Jesus did for you, as being saved from hell and given eternal life!*

Now that's worth getting excited over! You may have not come to God initially to be healed, but healing, according to Matthew 15:26, is "the children's bread."

Several years ago, my vehicle broke down right in front of my office. Staring at the car through my office window only made me more and more depressed. Money was a little tight in that season, so the thought of adding a towing charge on top of a repair bill felt a bit overwhelming. Within a few minutes, though, it came to my attention that the new insurance company I had recently signed up with included roadside assistance and towing. About thirty minutes later my vehicle was being towed to the local repair shop, and I found myself thanking the Lord for some extra benefits I didn't even know I had.

Healing is ours made possible through Jesus, but as Peter stated in the above-mentioned verse it is reserved for those "who believe." The Lord, speaking through the prophet Hosea, said in Hosea 4:6, "My people are destroyed for lack of knowledge." It wasn't until I realized that towing was included with my insurance that I could take advantage of it.

Sadly many Christians needlessly suffer at the hand of sickness only because they're unaware that they have a right to healing. Yes, they've received Jesus into their lives for the forgiveness of sins, but they have failed to realize that healing, along with other benefits, are included in their salvation package.

Several years ago, I watched my mom walk out her healing. She had been diagnosed with breast cancer and her doctors recommended all the normal treatments. Invasive surgery followed by chemotherapy and radiation left her tired, weak, and hairless. We were concerned for her as we watched those treatments take a toll on her body, yet despite her frailty her spirit grew strong. Mom had been a part of a couple of churches I had pastored through the years, and the message of sozo came alive in her.

When doctors weren't quite sure what her outcome was going to be, and as her body grew more tired and weak, her faith was coming alive on the inside day by day.

Mom grabbed ahold of the word of God and accepted as fact that Jesus had healed her on the cross and believed with all her heart that she was going to walk out of this situation completely healed. Soon her body began to line up with her faith, and the final report revealed what she had believed as she was completely cancer free and remains so to this day!

> *Mom grabbed ahold of the word of God and accepted as fact that Jesus had healed her on the cross and believed with all her heart that she was going to walk out of this situation completely healed.*

If you need healing today, know that just as it was God's will to save you, so it is also His will to heal you. Yes, I know that statement sounds bold, but it's true and Jesus even said so. When Jesus encountered a man who had been ravaged by leprosy, He made it clear what His will was concerning healing. Matthew 8:2-3 says, "A man with leprosy came and knelt before him and said, 'Lord, if you are willing, you can make me clean.' Jesus reached out his hand and touched the man. 'I am willing,' he said. 'Be clean!' Immediately he was cleansed of his leprosy" (NIV).

Jesus Christ on this earth was the exact replication and representation of the Father's heart. Jesus said in John 14:9, "Anyone who has seen me has seen the Father" (NIV). In John 10:30, Jesus said, "I and the Father are one" (NIV). In John 5:19 Jesus made it clear that He was the personification of His Father's heart when He said, "Very truly I tell you, the Son can do nothing by himself; he can do only what he sees his Father doing, because whatever the Father does the Son also does" (NIV).

If you need healing today of any kind and at any level, you can ask for and receive your healing by faith, knowing that it is indeed the Father's desire for you to be healed. Let's pray and agree together for your healing.

Father, in the name of Jesus I set my faith in agreement with the person reading this book who needs healing. I thank You, Father, that You sent Your Son, Jesus, to the cross not only for the forgiveness of sins, but also for our healing. I declare in accordance with Your Word by faith that my sister or brother is completely and totally healed from the top of their head to the souls of their feet. I declare complete healing over him or her in every area of their mind, body, and spirit, and we receive this now! In Jesus' name, Amen!!!

Chapter Three Study Guide Questions

Do you believe God still heals today? If so, do you see healing as something we hope God does for us if He feels like it, or as something that is already done through Jesus' finished work and included in our salvation package?

_____

_____

Have you experienced God's divine healing in an area? If so, list the area(s) below.

_____

_____

Why do you think people are sometimes hesitant to ask for and receive healing?

_____

_____

In what area(s) might you need to be healed that you've not yet seen the manifestation of healing?

_____

_____

Activate your faith! Through prayer and the taking of holy communion, receive your healing today!

_____

_____

Chapter Four:
Delivered

There's no better story in Scripture that depicts God's delivering power more than the one found in Mark 5:1-20 and Luke 8:26-39. In these two accounts we see a man who was so vexed and bound by demons that no one could help him—that was, until someone named Jesus came his way. Mark vividly describes this man's situation in verses 2-5:

When Jesus climbed out of the boat, a man possessed by an evil spirit came out from the tombs to meet him. This man lived in the burial caves and could no longer be restrained, even with a chain. Whenever he was put into chains and shackles—as he often was—he snapped the chains from his wrists and smashed the shackles. No one was strong enough to subdue him. Day and night he wandered among the burial caves and in the hills, howling and cutting himself with sharp stones (NLT).

Wow! This fellow was in a tough spot. I can't even imagine what that must have been like for him.

It's obvious by his display of supernatural strength and his behavior that something had ahold of him that was beyond natural. All of that changed, however, when this man encountered Jesus. It's worth noting also that this man ran to meet Jesus and fell at his feet. Yes, the demons had a lot of control over him, but they didn't have complete control. They couldn't control his will and desire. I'm not sure what door was open in this man's life to bring about such bondage, but by the way in which he approached Jesus he was clearly tired of it all. This man was ready to be delivered and set free. This is an important factor, because God doesn't deliver us from our friends, those things we want or like, but He will deliver us from our enemies.

> *God doesn't deliver us from our friends, those things we want or like, but He will deliver us from our enemies.*

Many Christians today are saved from their sins and on their way to heaven, but sadly still live in bondage of one kind or another. They may not be in the same place as this fellow, but they are enslaved nonetheless.

Many God-loving Christians find themselves bound by fear, worry, depression, alcoholism, drug addiction, pornography, and so on. Many believers know that the bondage they find themselves in is a direct contradiction to the Gospel they profess, yet they are still bound. Maybe you can relate. If so, your heavenly Father wants you to know there is deliverance for you, and it is one of the seven benefits of salvation.

Peter found himself in a pickle, to say the least, and needed deliverance. In Acts 5:12-17 we find Peter bound in prison and chained to multiple guards. There would be no fair trial for Peter either, and he knew that just like James he would most likely be put to death the very next day. Fortunately for Peter there was a group of believers praying for him. A bunch of them had gathered at a home in town and were crying out to God in earnest for Peter's safe deliverance. The Lord heard those prayers and answered them in a mighty way. An angel of the Lord went into that prison cell, slapped Peter awake as his chains fell off, then escorted Peter right out the front gate! Peter wasn't sure at first if it was all a dream, but he soon realized he had been set free. He hastily made his way to the prayer meeting only to get the door slammed in his face as Rhoda, the servant girl, couldn't believe her eyes. God had delivered Peter

Your New Identity

In Mark 10:46-52 we see the story of "Blind Bartimaeus." Who knows how long the spot on the side of the road, just outside the gates of Jericho, had been his home? His whole identity was wrapped up in that roadside spot and his lot of being a blind beggar. He wasn't even known by his own name for Bartimaeus literally means "son of Timaeus." He was known to everyone as, "The Blind Beggar, Son of Timaeus."

One day, however, he heard a great commotion and asked those around him what was going on. Someone replied, "Jesus of Nazareth is passing by." Those around Bartimaeus knew of Jesus based on the reputation of where He was from, Nazareth, but Bartimaeus somehow received a revelation as to who Jesus really was.

Bartimaeus shouted from the top of his lungs, "Jesus, Son of David, have mercy on me!" Bartimaeus' desire for deliverance was greater than the identity he had come to know.

He wanted to be delivered from this life of destitution, blindness, and begging. He wanted a fresh, new start and was willing to leave the old life behind. When Jesus called for Bartimaeus, the first thing he did was cast his dirty, worn beggar-coat aside. This was the coat everyone identified him with, and although soiled, tattered, and smelly Bartimaeus had grown accustomed to the coat and relied on it to help him eke out a meager living. He somehow knew in his heart that this encounter with Jesus was going to set him free and that he would never need the coat again.

Mark 10:51-52 says, "And Jesus answered and said unto him, 'What wilt thou that I should do unto thee?' The blind man said unto him, 'Lord, that I might receive my sight.' And Jesus said unto him, 'Go thy way; thy faith hath made thee whole'. And immediately he received his sight and followed Jesus in the way" (KJV).

By now, it may not surprise you to know that the word whole in verse 52 is the word sozo. Bartimaeus' willingness to let the old life go set him up to receive deliverance. Jesus delivered him from his life of destitution and revealed to him the true identity and destiny God had for him.

Have the circumstances of life left you feeling bound and imprisoned at times? If so, there is an answer. The same delivering power that set Peter, the demoniac man and Bartimaeus free can set you free. Maybe right now as you're reading this you're remembering some things God has delivered you from. I know I am! As you remember things or situations you know only God could have delivered you from, gratitude and thanksgiving fill your heart. But what you may have not realized is that the deliverance you have experienced or possibly still need, is all a part of your salvation package through Jesus.

> *The same delivering power that set Peter, the demoniac man and Bartimaeus free can set you free.*

Today if you find yourself in need of deliverance, can I pray with you?

Father, In the name of Jesus I set my faith in agreement with my brother or sister reading this book right now. I ask You, Father, to set them free from anything that may have them bound. Deliver them, Lord, right now through the resurrection power of Jesus! I thank You that deliverance is part of our salvation package, so I declare and decree that they are loosed and set free in Jesus' name, and I thank You that "he who the Son sets free is free indeed!" Amen!!!

Chapter Four Study Guide Questions

How would you define or describe deliverance?

_____

_____

How does it impact you to know that being delivered is just as much a part of being saved as is being forgiven?

_____

_____

Like Bartimaeus, have you ever found yourself cloaked in the wrong identity, living in a subpar place, far below the standard of the abundant life Jesus speaks of in John 10:10? If so, identify those areas below.

_____

_____

Like Bartimaeus, call out to Jesus, by revelation, as your Deliverer and receive, by faith, freedom from anything that has you bound. As the Holy Spirit helps you, write out a prayer receiving your deliverance.

_____

_____

Chapter Five:

Preserved

When I hear the word preserved, my mind goes back to my grandmother's kitchen. Growing up in the South it used to be common for people to can and preserve foods. My grandparents would grow a garden and when they couldn't eat all they had planted they would put away food through canning and preserving. You certainly don't see this as much as you used to, although some still practice this art of preserving.

My grandmother could can a jar of beans and when you ate them in the winter they had just as much flavor as the day she picked them.

Even now, when I think about my grandma's peach or pear preserves and how you could spread a spoonful of them on a piece of toast or a biscuit, it makes my mouth water.

Preserved can be defined as "to keep alive, or in existence; make lasting, to keep safe from harm or injury; protect or spare." Preserved, by its definition, can sound a lot like "delivered and protected."

> Preserved can be defined as "to keep alive, or in existence; make lasting, to keep safe from harm or injury; protect or spare."

In essence you could say they are triplets. Yet, as you see in the definition, to preserve something is for a purpose, and that purpose can be for a specific use. Like my grandma's preserved goodies that were reserved for use in the winter, so our heavenly Father preserves us for the purposes and plans He has for us. In Jeremiah 29:11 God says: "'For I know the plans I have for you,' declares the LORD, 'plans to prosper you and not to harm you, plans to give you hope and a future'" (NIV).

Power to Preserve

No story in scripture illustrates God's power to preserve more than the story of Joash found in Second Chronicles.

Joash's evil grandmother had all the heirs to the throne killed in an effort to rule the land herself. However, she overlooked Joash who was just an infant and the only bloodline of King David left on earth. A relative formed a plan to hide Joash in an inner room in the temple where he remained, along with his nurse, for six years. Can you imagine what that must have been like for Joash and his nurse? Throughout those six long years of solitary confinement, God's divine plan must have seemed like a prison.

Yet, at the right time Joash was brought out of that room and coronated as king to fulfill the plans of the Lord for the house of David, the nation of Israel, and all of us, as the Messiah Himself would one day be a descendent of Joash. Through his divine plan, God also used Joash to later restore the Temple that had become dilapidated through the years.

The reason you're still here today is because God has preserved you for the plans and purposes He has for you! We see this in the life of Paul.

> *The reason you're still here today is because God has preserved you for the plans and purposes He has for you!*

Many people tried to snuff out his life, but none prevailed until God's plans and purpose for Paul were completed. There were also many attempts on David's life. Goliath tried to kill him, Saul tried to kill him, and even his own son Absalom tried to kill him, but God preserved David's life until His plan for him was completed. David accomplished a lot in his lifetime, and he made many mistakes along the way, but the Lord preserved David until his work was finished and he passed the baton onto Solomon.

Doesn't that encourage you? To know that you are still here, when so many others may not be, means that God still has His plans and purposes for you in mind. Can you look back and see how the Lord, in His goodness, has preserved you? Maybe you didn't realize until now, but preservation has been a part of your sozo salvation package all along.

Paul makes this clear in I Thessalonians 5:23 when he says, "Now may the God of peace Himself sanctify you completely; and may your whole spirit, soul, and body be preserved blameless at the coming of our Lord Jesus Christ".

Chapter Five Study Guide Questions

List some ways in which you know God has kept you and preserved you.

_____

_____

What are some things that you believe God has called you to do or walk in that you've yet to experience? Identify below some things that you believe God has preserved you for.

_____

_____

When you consider that you are still here and that God has indeed preserved you until this moment, how does that impact your everyday life?

_____

_____

Chapter Six:

Protected

As I mentioned previously, deliverance, preservation, and protection can have a lot of crossover similarities while each one also serves its own specific purpose and need. You could certainly say that Daniel was delivered, preserved, and protected in the lions' den. You could also say the same for the three young Hebrew men Shadrach, Meshack, and Abednego as they were all delivered, preserved, and protected in and from the fiery furnace. "Protection," however, is specifically defined as "to defend or guard from attack, invasion, loss, annoyance, insult, etc.; to cover or shield from injury or danger."

> *"Protection," however, is specifically defined as "to defend or guard from attack, invasion, loss, annoyance, insult, etc.; to cover or shield from injury or danger."*

There have been countless times throughout my life that I know, without a doubt, God protected me, as I'm sure you can say the same for your own life. At various times, God has protected me from physical harm and danger, wrong relationships, and bad decisions. He has even protected my heart and reputation. What I've learned through the years is, just as any good father wants to protect his children, so our heavenly Father desires to be our protection even more.

> *Just as any good father wants to protect his children, so our heavenly Father desires to be our protection even more.*

Surrounded by poverty, Dalys grew up in a middle-class home in Panama. Her mother and father worked hard to provide for her and her siblings, and at times she saw her dad reach deep into his own pocket to help families and children throughout their community. Although beautiful, Dalys had not found the "love of her life" she had been hoping for. Through a friend Dalys met an American guy who had come to Panama for work, but really at the top of his list was to find a wife.

Their acquaintance soon became a relationship, and before long this gentleman asked Dalys for her hand in marriage. Although Dalys couldn't say she was madly in love with him, now in her late twenties, she desired a family of her own and knew her clock was ticking.

Her father had fallen ill, and fearing his passing, Dalys sought for his blessing on the marriage. He gave it to her, but with reservation. Something about the situation didn't quite seem right to her dad and some other family members. Yet, everyone was hopeful that Dalys had found true love and would have her own "happily ever after."

Dalys married, moved to the U.S., and tried hard to assimilate into American culture. A new family, a new language, and a new country felt overwhelming at times, but Dalys sought the Lord's help and relied on His guidance to help her be the best wife she could be. Although the marriage started out well, over the years dysfunction became the norm. They were never in one place for long, as her husband couldn't settle down and moved from one job to another, never seeming to find his place. All the dysfunction reached a tipping point, and the marriage Dalys wanted, and had waited for so long, fell apart.

Now living all alone Dalys felt unprotected, and this feeling was made worse when some random man tried to violently break in to her home one night.

Seeking protection, Dalys decided to get a dog but not just any dog. She got the biggest Doberman she could find. Dalys took pride in her big dog and felt completely safe, as if nothing could ever harm her with him by her side. Eventually, Dalys moved from South Dakota to Florida. She had diligently saved to make this move, and the company she worked for allowed her to transfer her employment to one of their Florida agencies. Now all Dalys needed to do was find a place to live. A Motel 6 was her temporary home while she went from one apartment complex to another filling out applications.

At first Dalys didn't realize the motel she was staying at was in a rough part of town, until she noticed the drug and prostitution traffic surrounding her at all hours of the day and night. This made her evermore grateful she had her big Doberman to protect her! Even though she was only about five feet four in stature, as she daily made her way in and out of the motel complex no one dared bother her so long as her Doberman was by her side.

Dalys was making no progress on her search for an apartment. Although she had put in applications at almost every apartment complex in the area and even up to a thirty-minute drive away, no one was calling her back. She had money in savings and a great credit score, but no one wanted to rent to her. She finally came to the realization that this was because of her Doberman.

In desperation and with tears running down her face Dalys cried out to the Lord for help. As she knelt across the bed weeping and praying, she heard the still, small loving voice of the Lord loud and clear. "Dalys, don't you think I can protect you more than your dog? Don't you think I can provide for you more than that money you have in the bank? Let Me be your protection and provision," the Lord said. Dalys accepted that invitation from the Lord to be her source, and completely and totally surrendered herself to Him. Dalys made the decision to give up her Doberman for adoption, and he soon found a family and a home he could thrive in. Soon after, Dalys found an apartment to call home and a new life she never imagined was possible.

Our Father wants to be our Protector. Take some time to meditate on these verse that speak on God's divine protection.

But the Lord is faithful, and he will strengthen you and protect you from the evil one. (2 Thessalonians 3:3 NIV)

So do not fear, for I am with you; do not be dismayed, for I am your God. I will strengthen you and help you; I will uphold you with my righteous right hand. (Isaiah 41:10 NIV)

But let all who take refuge in you be glad; let them ever sing for joy. Spread your protection over them, that those who love your name may rejoice in you. (Psalm 5:11 NIV)

May the LORD answer you when you are in distress; may the name of the God of Jacob protect you. (Psalm 20:1 NIV)

Keep me safe, LORD, from the hands of the wicked; protect me from the violent, who devise ways to trip my feet. (Psalm 140:4 NIV)

Do you, for some reason or circumstance, feel unprotected? If so, can we pray and agree together?

Father, I ask You in Jesus' name to wrap Your arms of protection around the person reading this right now. I pray that You would surround them with Your presence and fill them with the certainty that You care deeply about where they are and how they feel. May they see and know that You are ever watching over them and protecting them and because You are their source for protection they have no need to fear. Fill them, Father, with the peace that only You can give right now, in Jesus' name! Amen!!!

Chapter Six Study Guide Questions

Reflecting on your life and experiences, list some ways in which you know God has protected you.

_____

_____

Has God's protection over your life ever come through unanswered prayers or prayers that weren't answered the way you wanted in the moment? If so, how does that make you feel, knowing that the unanswered prayer was indeed divine protection?

_____

_____

How does knowing God's protection is part of our salvation package impact your life moving forward?

_____

_____

Chapter Seven:

Make Prosperous

Much controversy has surrounded the concept of godly prosperity through the years. Because of exaggerations and excesses, some Christians have decided to "throw the baby out with the bath water" when it comes to prosperity. Many have adopted the thinking that God really doesn't care if we are prosperous or not, and that He is way more concerned about our spiritual condition than our well-being.

The truth is, this way of thinking couldn't be farther from the truth. It's not an either/or for Him. Our heavenly Father cares deeply about every area of our lives, and that includes provision and prosperity.

> *Our heavenly Father cares deeply about every area of our lives, and that includes provision and prosperity.*

There are many verses and stories throughout Scripture where God expresses and demonstrates His care for our provision and prosperity. One such verse is 3 John 2, which says, "Beloved, I pray that you may prosper in all things and be in health, just as your soul prospers." Sadly, some have reduced this verse down to just a greeting in a letter from a writer to a recipient. But given the truth that all Scripture is inspired by the Holy Spirit, this verse should be taken to be a representation of the Father's heart and desire for us.

One way in which our adversary attempts to get us to reject God's provision and prosperity is in how he tries to get us to perceive it. And the best way to counter this is to see prosperity in the light of God's truth. Bible prosperity properly defined is "to be fully supplied, in need or want of nothing."

When you look at prosperity from that perspective, it makes more sense. Think about it. As a parent do you want your child in need or want? Of course not! Then why should we think anything less of our heavenly Father? Even as a kid in school you could recognize a child who was in need or want. And when you did, you probably thought that child most likely came from a needy home with parents who were unable to provide well.

Our heavenly Father wants to provide greatly for us, and He's well able to do so! Philippians 4:19 says, "And this same God who takes care of me will supply all your needs from his glorious riches, which have been given to us in Christ Jesus" (NLT). How has God provided for us through Christ Jesus? He did so on the cross. Second Corinthians 8:9 says, "For you know the grace of our Lord Jesus Christ, that though he was rich, yet for your sake he became poor, so that you through his poverty might become rich" (NIV). This word "rich" is not speaking of spiritual riches. It is defined in the Greek as "to have abundance of outward possessions, and to be richly supplied."

It's been said that God is more concerned about what you hold in your heart than what you have in your hand. I've had some well-off friends throughout my life, but their wealth never really impressed me. What impressed me was how I watched some of them walk it out. It wasn't what they had, but how they handled it. I've watched as some of them kept their hunger and passion for the Lord, remained humble and relatable to others around them, and gave cheerfully as the Lord led them to give. Our heavenly Father wants to be our source for provision and prosperity, and He wants us to remain aware that true prosperity comes from Him.

The Apostle Paul knew God to be his source and strength and he knew that in trusting God he could be content. Philippians 4:11-13 says, "I am not saying this because I am in need, for I have learned to be content whatever the circumstances. I know what it is to be in need, and I know what it is to have plenty. I have learned the secret of being content in any and every situation, whether well fed or hungry, whether living in plenty or in want. I can do all this through him who gives me strength" (NIV).

I've experienced many seasons of abundance and sometimes lack in life. I will never forget this one lean season I was in years ago when Christmas was right around the corner. Money was so tight I didn't know how I was going to get presents that year and I really wanted to make Christmas special for my little girl. After spending four years in the Marine Corps, I started a carpet-cleaning business, which I operated for about ten years.

In an effort to expand my business, I started franchising it in eastern North Carolina and had sold a few franchises when I decided to buy out a Raleigh-based carpet-cleaning business that shared the same name.

My business had grown and done well through the years, and upon moving to Raleigh I set out to aggressively grow the business even more. The truth is, I got way too aggressive and before I knew it, I was in way over my head. I had rented a large office building, bought more carpet-cleaning vans and equipment, and was spending thousands of dollars a month in advertising.

Things had gotten so tight I found myself putting expenses and even payroll on credit cards. I was at the brink of bankruptcy when I fell to my knees and prayed for the Lord to guide me out of this self-inflicted situation. He responded by giving me the wisdom I desperately needed. He led me to downsize the business and at the same time sell my house to use the substantial equity to pay off all my bills and debt, which I did. My buyer was the co-pastor at the church I attended, and while his family moved into my house we moved into the singlewide two-bedroom mobile home he had just moved out of. I felt immediate relief as the financial pressure was subsiding.

As fall and the holidays were approaching, the church I was attending was about to receive their big annual offering they called "The Chest of Joash."

They used this offering every year for their buildings and facilities, and through this offering all the church facilities were completely paid for and well maintained. Seeing that it was my first year at the church, I really wanted to be a part of this offering. But after paying off all my bills and debts, I only had five hundred dollars remaining, which I was holding onto tightly for Christmas. My little girl wanted a puppy and I wanted to get her one.

The pastor asked us all to pray about what the Lord would have us give, and he encouraged us to do whatever the Lord led us to do. I prayed, and to my dismay I felt the Lord leading me to give that five hundred dollars I was holding onto. He was inviting me to trust Him and allow Him to be my provision, so I did. When that special Sunday morning rolled around, there was lots of excitement and anticipation in the air. This was a big deal, and the worship service was filled with worship and celebration unto the Lord. At the end of the service people came forward and one by one dropped their offering in the beautifully decorated chest that had been placed up front where the communion table usually sat. I felt joy and peace fill my heart as I dropped that five hundred dollars in the chest. It was all that I had to give, yet I knew I could trust the Lord with it and that somehow He would provide.

As I made my way out of the church sanctuary and opened the door to enter the large lobby, an older couple was standing there looking at me with amazement. Aside from recognizing this couple as faithful attenders, I really didn't know them well at all. The wife reached out and grabbed my arm and said, "We've been looking for you!" To which I replied, "Really?"

Her husband responded, "Yes, brother. The Lord has laid you on our hearts and we want to bless you." Then he handed me an envelope. I graciously thanked them and made my way to the car. I opened the envelope and to my shock and surprise there were five crisp one-hundred-dollar bills. The exact amount of money I had just given to the Lord as an act of worship to Him. The Lord reminded me right there once again that He was well able to be my provider, my provision, and my prosperity.

> *Our heavenly Father wants us to know that He cares about our prosperity*

Our heavenly Father wants us to know that He cares about our prosperity.

No, not everyone is going to live in a mansion overlooking the sea or drive a Rolls-Royce, but He does want us to be fully supplied, in need or want of nothing.

And when we find ourselves in need, He wants us to turn to Him as our source. Think about the fact that something we consider so precious, gold, God uses as street pavement in Heaven. How cruel would it be for any parent to have that much provision only to watch their children suffer and be in lack? That is not our heavenly Father! He loves us deeply and wants to provide for us and has done so through the finished work of Jesus on the cross.

Do you find yourself in a place of lack or need today? If so, know that through Jesus our heavenly Father has and will supply everything we need, we must just simply believe and receive by faith. This verse in Romans 8:32 bears repeating: "He who did not spare his own Son, but gave him up for us all—how will he not also, along with him, graciously give us all things?" (NIV).

May I pray with you concerning any financial need you may be facing today?

Father, in Jesus' name I ask You to meet every need my brother or sister may be facing today! I thank You, Father, that Your desire for us, Your children, is that we are fully supplied, in need or want of nothing. I declare financial wholeness today over my sister or brother and thank You that You have met and are still meeting their need in abundance. Thank You, Father, for being our source for provision and prosperity. In Jesus' mighty name, Amen!!!

Chapter Seven Study Guide Questions

What is the first thing that comes to mind when you hear the word prosper?

_____
_____

Do you, at times, find it hard to accept that your heavenly Father wants to prosper you? What do you think makes it difficult to accept God's divine provision?

_____
_____

Find three scriptures that speak of God's desire to prosper us and write them below.

_____
_____

Chapter Eight:
Make Whole

If you walk down the streets of any city or town in Israel, a passerby may greet you with the word "shalom." It happened to me on my first trip to Israel. As I was passing a gentleman, I said, "Hello," to which he replied, "Shalom." I thought this was such a neat thing that when I saw a placard that said "Shalom Y'all" in one of the gift shops, being from the South, I just had to buy it. For most Israelis this word is much more than a greeting. Stemming from their long line of rich Hebrew heritage, this word shalom is a blessing.

> *this word shalom is a blessing*

When they pass each other in the market, on the streets, or in the halls, they are pronouncing a blessing over one another, and for most of them they believe this blessing carries real weight and meaning.

This Hebrew word shalom is translated into the English word "peace." But to get the fullness of its meaning you must go deeper. The actual definition of shalom is "peace, well, welfare, prosperity, safety, health and completeness."

The word "completeness" in this definition can be defined as "wholeness," which itself is defined as "nothing missing, and nothing broken." The Hebrew word shalom is as close to the word saved or the Greek word sozo as possible. Jesus said in John 14:27, "Peace I leave with you; my peace I give you. I do not give to you as the world gives. Do not let your hearts be troubled and do not be afraid" (NIV).

When Jesus used this word "peace," He was including with it all of the things shalom included, plus more. He added some extra meanings that only those living in the age of the New Covenant could know and receive.

> *When Jesus used this word "peace," He was including with it all of the things shalom included, plus more.*

This word "peace" in Greek is the word eirene and has the following expanded definition: "the tranquil state of a soul assured of its salvation through Christ, and so fearing nothing from God."

In essence Jesus was telling all His followers, including you and me, that we had nothing to fear from God and could rest in the assurance that everything was good between us and the Father. As Jesus was departing for Heaven, He wanted us to know that we could be at peace because there was nothing missing and nothing broken.

Jesus went out of His way one day to personally deliver this peace to a Samaritan woman who desperately needed it. John's Gospel gives us the play-by-play. Jesus, tired and thirsty from a long walk, came to Jacob's Well. This was no random stop, however. Because Jesus always followed the leading of His Father, He was sent there on a mission. This woman had been on the hunt for peace for years, as was evidenced by her many failed relationships. Jesus "read her mail," letting her know that He knew she had been married five times and was currently shacked up with a sixth guy. He didn't do this to condemn her but to let her know that He knew all about her yet still accepted her. This would be the peace she had always longed for!

There weren't many people to whom Jesus just came right out and revealed that He was the Messiah, but He did with this Samaritan woman. In essence, Jesus was bringing to light all her efforts to be unconditionally loved and accepted, and letting her know that she was — by the greatest Person who ever walked the face of the earth. She would never again have to avoid making eye contact with people in the marketplace. She would never again have to draw water from that well in the heat of the day to avoid all the glares of the neighborhood women. She had finally found her Everlasting Love, and He gave her Everlasting Water that would forever quench her thirsty soul.

The Lord prophetically spoke to me about writing this book way back in the summer of 2000. So, what took so long? Well, although I've spoken about sozo countless times, there's something about writing a book that's different. For some reason folks seem to think that when you write a book on a particular topic that you're an expert in that area. Let me be clear that I am by no means an expert when it comes to all of the wonders and depths of salvation. It's not that I had been deliberately avoiding writing this book, but God had me put it on the shelf until His timing was right. Once I finally had the "green light" to write it, I felt the Lord say to me, "You can't write the book while I'm still writing your chapters."

For many years I could attest to having personally experienced five or so of the seven benefits of sozo (saved, healed, delivered, preserved, protected, made prosperous, made whole). But there always seemed to be a couple of sozo benefits that eluded me. To be honest, the Lord has had to do a work in and through my life on a personal level to bring me into a place of wholeness. He didn't want me to write about something I had not yet experienced for myself, and I'm grateful for that!

Today, through the grace of God, I can truly say I am walking in a place of wholeness that I've never known before and am grateful that His grace continues to work in and through me.

If you, like me, have found wholeness to be an arm's length away let me encourage you to keep believing and trusting in God for what you need.

Just because there may be areas of sozo we have yet to experience, doesn't mean they're not true and truly meant for us. Your heavenly Father wants you to live and enjoy a life of wholeness that only He can bring, a life that Jesus speaks of in John 10:10 when He says, "I have come that they may have life, and that they may have it more abundantly."

> *Just because there may be areas of sozo we have yet to experience, doesn't mean they're not true and truly meant for us.*

Is there anything still missing or broken in your life for which you need the wholeness and peace that only Jesus can give? If so, please allow me to pray with you.

Father, I come before You with my sister or brother asking You, in the name of Jesus, to make them completely whole. Father, I pray that Your shalom and sozo peace would come upon them and that through Your mighty power that was displayed through Jesus on the cross, You would make them whole in every way. I pray, Father, right now that he or she would receive that wholeness and truly see the "goodness of the Lord in the land of the living." I boldly ask and declare Your blessing upon their life in Jesus' mighty name, Amen!!!

Chapter Eight Study Guide Questions

Identify below any areas you feel are not whole in your life?

_____

_____

How does Jesus' interaction with the woman at the well speak to you?

_____

_____

Considering the truth of sozo, do you feel the Lord would have you settle for areas of your life that are not whole, or does He want you to pursue Him for complete wholeness? How will you move toward complete wholeness?

_____

_____

Using a concordance, or BlueLetterBible.org, look up the word peace found in John 14:27 and write down all its definitions. How does the definition of the peace that Jesus gives us help you?

_____

_____

Chapter Nine:

Taste and See

Google reviews are all the rage these days. Business owners know that it doesn't take many bad reviews to impact their business negatively, while at the same time a five-star review is like gold. I've found myself reading reviews more often these days, especially about restaurants I've never been to before. A credible review for a restaurant is one from a patron who's frequented the establishment. Anyone can have a good or bad experience with one visit, but when a "regular" who has tried just about everything on the menu says it's great, then it's usually great.

David was a "regular" when it came to tasting the Lord's goodness. He had gone to the Lord countless times throughout his life and never once was he disappointed. In every case and occasion David had always been able to count on the Lord.

When rejected by his father and brothers by being left to tend the sheep when Samuel came to anoint the next king of Israel, David tasted acceptance as that precious anointing oil ran down his face from his head. When mocked by his brothers for being puny, David tasted the supernatural might of the Lord that gave him victory over Goliath. When David found himself running from Saul, he tasted the protection and preservation of the Lord. When David had an adulterous affair and murdered her husband, he tasted the forgiveness and mercy of the Lord.

Most believers have never tasted all the benefits of their salvation package found in sozo, simply because they're not aware of all Jesus did for them on the cross. And although they may never say so with words, their faces and the lack of joy on their countenance give God an undeserved bad review. Now that you've discovered what Sozo Living is all about, why don't you taste and see for yourself just how good God is?

> *Most believers have never tasted all the benefits of their salvation package found in sozo, simply because they're not aware of all Jesus did for them on the cross.*

A Clear Picture of Sozo

The Old Testament is filled with types and shadows that point to New Testament, or New Covenant, truths. It's been said that the Old Testament is the Good News concealed while the New Testament is the Good News revealed. One such type and shadow is found in the story of the Hebrews' exodus from Egypt. You know the story. God sent Moses to deliver the Israelites from the cruel hand of Pharoah, but Pharoah refused to let them go. Nine plagues had left Egypt in utter ruins, yet Pharoah's heart remained hard.

God would use the tenth and final plague to free His children from Pharoah's grip.

The Lord gave clear instruction as to what to do, and the word was quickly spread among the Hebrews. The Lord told them to handpick a young unblemished lamb and bring it into their homes, taking care of it for four days. Can you imagine how they must have grown attached to those precious little lambs in their homes? But after the fourth day they were to slay the lamb and pour out its blood in a basin. Then they were to fasten some hyssop together, forming a type of brush, and then paint the lamb's blood at the top and on both sides of the main doorpost of their homes.

Then they were to roast the lamb with bitter herbs and eat every bite. If the family was too small to eat a whole lamb, they were to share it with another family, but all the lamb's meat must be consumed. On that faithful night as the "Death Angel" passed by each home throughout all of Egypt, every firstborn male, human or animal, died. Only the homes on which the blood was applied were spared. The recognition of this night has been celebrated among Jews for thousands of years as the Feast of Passover. As the sounds of wailing filled the cities, Moses led the Hebrews out of Egypt where they had been enslaved for four hundred years.

This miraculous event is a picture of salvation for you and me living in this age of grace. As Egypt is a type and shadow of the world, and the Hebrews a type and shadow of the Church, we as believers are saved from the world and its

> *This miraculous event is a picture of salvation for you and me living in this age of grace.*

deserved judgment by the blood of the Lamb, Jesus Christ. Aren't you glad to be saved?!?!

But David goes on to paint an even clearer picture of what happened that night. Psalm 105:37 says, "The LORD brought his people out of Egypt, loaded with silver and gold; and not one among the tribes of Israel even stumbled" (NLT). If you remember the story, you'll recall that Moses instructed the Hebrews to go throughout the land of Egypt and ask the Egyptians for treasures. By the time those Egyptians had been through those plagues, I'm sure they would have been glad to give those Hebrews anything they wanted. In fact, they gave them so much treasure that the Israelites were "loaded."

On top of that, Psalm 105:37 says that as they came out of Egypt, "not one among the tribes of Israel even stumbled." What exactly does that mean? you may wonder. The King James Version says it this way: "and there was not one feeble person among their tribes." This word "feeble" is defined as "weak, cripple, or faint."

Now this picture is getting even clearer! You see, sometime during that Passover night as the blood from the lambs were applied to the door and the meat roasted and consumed, healing happened. The Hebrews left Egypt saved from death and fully supplied, in need or want of nothing.

Perceive and Receive

Our ability to receive from God has much to do with how we perceive God. Our perception of Him can often determine how little or much we receive from Him.

> *Our ability to receive from God has much to do with how we perceive God.*

It's been said that "perception is reality." So, the question is, how do you perceive God?

I can tell you that in my early years of growing up in church, my perception of God was much different than it is today.

Don't get me wrong. I'm thankful for my Christian upbringing. But the strong religious environment in which I was raised painted a wrong and even schizophrenic picture of God on the walls of my mind. I grew up never knowing when and if God was pleased with me.

On the day I prayed, read my Bible, or did some good deed I felt as though God might be pleased. But most days I wasn't quite sure. Most of the sermons I heard left me feeling like I was never doing enough. Never serving enough. Never reading God's Word enough. Never praying enough. Never serving enough. I lived in the "you need to's." "You need to do this," or "you need to do that" for God to be pleased.

I loved the Lord and had accepted Jesus as my Savior, but my picture and perception of God was all wrong.

If you had asked me to honestly describe to you what I thought God looked like, I would have described a scoured –faced father-time-looking kind of character. A bald, grey, grumpy-looking old man who was always ready to thump me on the head whenever I did something wrong. Sadly, many Christians have had that same wrong religious perception.

A True Picture of the Father

I'm sure you would agree that everything Jesus did was perfect. When He healed it was perfect! When He opened blinded eyes, it was perfect!

When He turned water into wine it was perfect! Everything He did was absolutely perfect, and when He told a large group of people the story of the prodigal son, He painted a perfect picture of our heavenly Father.

The picture Jesus painted was shocking to the hearers, because the way in which He described the Father in that story violated all customs and norms.

It was uncustomary for a Hebrew father to show great emotion by running to one of his children and embracing him with a kiss, especially a child who had caused such shame, disgrace, and dishonor. Yet, the picture Jesus painted was that of a father who loved his son so much, that despite the son's insult, abandonment, and sin, he welcomed him back with open, loving arms. And not only was this wayward son forgiven, but he was completely restored to full sonship and celebrated.

How do you perceive God today? He wants you to see Him as the always loving heavenly Father that He is and will always, unconditionally, remain. As you perceive Him rightly, receive from Him everything He has provided for you through Jesus.

Chapter Nine Study Guide Questions

When you think of God, what picture comes to mind?

_____
_____

Write down the characteristics of the father Jesus describes in the story of the prodigal son.

_____
_____

Have any wrong perceptions of God kept you from receiving good things from Him? If so, identify those areas below and list the truth of how you know, based on New Testament teaching, God would want you to see Him.

_____
_____

Chapter Ten:
How to Receive

Hopefully you've been reading this book with an open heart and mind and the Holy Spirit has stirred within you a desire for more, if not all, of what Jesus Christ has provided for you through His finished work on the cross. So how do you receive more and all? The answer is found in two ways. The first is found in the same way you most likely came to Christ in the beginning.

> *You confessed with your mouth and believed in your heart. Just as you called upon the name of the Lord to save you from your sin, in the same way you can call upon His name to receive the rest of your salvation package, sozo.*

You confessed with your mouth and believed in your heart. Just as you called upon the name of the Lord to save you from your sin, in the same way you can call upon His name to receive the rest of your salvation package, sozo.

Romans 10:9-10 says, "If you declare with your mouth, 'Jesus is Lord,' and believe in your heart that God raised him from the dead, you will be saved. For it is with your heart that you believe and are justified, and it is with your mouth that you profess your faith and are saved." Note, that the word "saved" in this verse is the word sozo.

All in the Name!

In the Old Testament God became known to His people through His character and deeds. For example, the first time we see the name Jehovah Jireh used was when Abraham called God by that name when God provided a lamb to be slain in place of his son Isaac. The name Jehovah means "God is." In essence Abraham was saying that God is, or has become, his provider. From what I can gather there are as many as nineteen different names in the Bible that describe God, including:

Yahweh - "The Lord is God"
Elohim - God the Creator
Abba – Father, or Daddy
Jehovah Jireh - "The Lord will provide"
Jehovah Rapha - "The God who heals"

Jehovah Nissi - "The Lord is my banner of protection"
Jehovah Shalom - "The Lord is peace"
Yahweh-Tsidkenu - "The Lord Our Righteousness"

No Other Name

Acts 4:11-12 says, "Jesus is 'the stone you builders rejected, which has become the cornerstone.' Salvation is found in no one else, for there is no other name under heaven given to mankind by which we must be saved" (NIV). This one verse makes it crystal clear! While it's great to know all the Old Testament names of God, there is only one name we must know today to be saved.

> *While it's great to know all the Old Testament names of God, there is only one name we must know today to be saved.*

Note that once again the word "saved" in the above verse is the Greek word sozo. Everything God ever was, as described in all His names, He is to us now through the one person Jesus Christ.

Jesus is Lord and Paul said in Romans 10:13 that, "Everyone who calls on the name of the Lord will be saved" (NLT). So today, or any day, as you call upon the name of Jesus you can do so by faith, receiving from Him anything you need that our heavenly Father has provided through Him. According to 2 Peter 1:3 Jesus is "everything we need for a godly life" (NIV).

The Meal That Heals

God gave us five senses, and the more of them we can include in an activity or something we are experiencing, the better. For example, when you sit down to enjoy a delicious steak dinner you are utilizing your sight, smell, and taste. It's one thing to hear something, but when you can add to that touch and taste, you're able to take it to a new level.

Such is the case with communion, the second way to receive all that Jesus has accomplished for us on the cross.

Jesus in His goodness left something we could always do, anytime we wanted to or needed to, to help us

> *Jesus in His goodness left something we could always do, anytime we wanted to or needed to, to help us receive from Him.*

receive from Him. How fitting that He introduced this to the disciples on the night of Passover just before He went to the cross.

Going back to the story of the Hebrews, there were two components God instituted that night for their salvation, healing, and deliverance from Egypt—the bodies and blood of the lamb. The meat of the lamb was eaten, and the bones were burned so that the lamb was completely consumed. Jesus knew that there would be times when we would need more than just words, though words spoken in faith are powerful. He knew we would need something from time to time we could touch, feel, taste, and completely consume, so He gave us the ability to have beautiful communion with Him through the bread and the cup. First Corinthians 10:16 says, "The cup of blessing which we bless, is it not the communion of the blood of Christ? The bread which we break, is it not the communion of the body of Christ?"

The word "communion" in the verse above is the Greek word koinonia, which is defined as "fellowship, association, community, joint participation, intercourse." You may not have been expecting to see that final word in the definition, but God uses that word to describe the intimacy we can experience with the Lord. He likens our communion with Him to the deepest physical intimacy that husband and wife are given to enjoy.

Now don't go getting weird on me. If God created intimacy between husband and wife, and then wants to use that to illustrate to us how He feels about communion, then that ought to be okay.

At the very least you could say that when we rightly partake in communion, it can be one of the closest things we can do to experience oneness with the Lord. Just as the Lord walked with Adam and Eve in the Garden in the cool of the day, so we can fellowship with Him through the body and blood of Jesus.

> *When we rightly partake in communion, it can be one of the closest things we can do to experience oneness with the Lord.*

This is where our adversary comes in. Just as he despised Adam and Eve's privilege of walking with God and enjoying fellowship with Him in the Garden, so he hates the thought of you and I enjoying fellowship and oneness with the Lord through communion. And as the "father of lies" he has used erroneous, religious teaching to rob us of this precious gift.

We've been told that if we take communion in an "unworthy manner," with any ounce of sin in our lives, known or unknown, that we may be in danger of death. Hearing that while growing up scared the beegeebees out of me, and sometimes I was almost too afraid to take communion. When I took it and didn't die on the spot, I figured I must have confessed everything "known or unknown" properly. Sadly, many believers have felt the same way and therefore take communion in fear and not faith. Let's look at the verses Paul wrote concerning communion from a different light, the light of truth.

First Corinthians 11:27-32 says, "So then, whoever eats the bread or drinks the cup of the Lord in an unworthy manner will be guilty of sinning against the body and blood of the Lord. Everyone ought to examine themselves before they eat of the bread and drink from the cup. For those who eat and drink without discerning the body of Christ eat and drink judgment on themselves. That is why many among you are weak and sick, and a number of you have fallen asleep. But if we were more discerning with regard to ourselves, we would not come under such judgment. Nevertheless, when we are judged in this way by the Lord, we are being disciplined so that we will not be finally condemned with the world" (NIV).

Let's break this down starting with the words "whoever eats the bread or drinks the cup of the Lord in an unworthy manner." The key word here is "manner" and not "man." He didn't say if we drink the cup and eat the bread as an unworthy man, but "manner."

The focus is not on the person eating or drinking but, in the way, or "manner," in which they partake of the bread and cup.

So how do we do it in a correct or worthy "manner?" In verse 28 Paul said we must "examine" ourselves. This word "examine" is from the Greek word dokimazo and means to "recognize as genuine after examination, to approve, deem worthy." This word

> *The right manner is to recognize and consider ourselves rightly in the body of Christ and in doing so count ourselves worthy and approved because we are in Him.*

"examine" is also used as a mathematical or accounting word to describe the act of counting something. So, it's not about the man, but the manner. The right manner is to recognize and consider ourselves rightly in the body of Christ and in doing so count ourselves worthy and approved because we are in Him.

When the sacrificial lambs were brought out to the priest for sacrifice, the priest did not examine the man, but the lamb. He did this to confirm that the lamb was perfect, with no blemish or defect. Then the man would place his hands on the lamb's head, representing the sin of him and his family.

The innocent lamb was then slain as punishment for their sins. In the Old Testament every year one man would be selected to place his hands on the head of an examined lamb for the forgiveness of sin to represent the entire nation. Jews still celebrate this feast called Yom Kippur.

Because some in the Corinthian church were not drawing a distinction between themselves and the rest of the world, and not considering themselves as rightly in the body of Christ, they were not able to receive communion by faith. As a result, they were falling victim to the same sickness, judgment, and even death as the rest of the world. Communion was doing them no good because they weren't considering themselves approved and worthy by placing themselves in the Lamb of God, Jesus, and they were thus receiving holy communion in an "unworthy manner."

If you flip this around it's easy to see that if we rightly discern who we are in Christ and receive communion in a

> *As a result of receiving communion in a worthy manner we should experience healing and wholeness.*

"worthy manner," then the opposite should happen. As a result of receiving communion in a worthy manner we should experience healing and wholeness.

Finally let's look at verse 32, which says, "Nevertheless, when we are judged in this way by the Lord, we are being disciplined so that we will not be finally condemned with the world." The word "judged" here means approved and the word "disciplined" means to train. This same verse could be translated, "Nevertheless, when we are approved in this way by the Lord, we are being trained so that we will not be finally condemned with the world." Wow doesn't that make a difference?!?!

Jesus said as often as we did this, communion, to do so remembering what He did for us on the cross and to declare it until He returns. So how often should we take communion? As often as you need or want, it's totally up to you. And we can serve communion to ourselves anytime and anyplace if we do so in a "worthy manner" so that the communion we take will have an impact in our lives. The early church took communion daily from house to house and at least weekly on the

Lord's Day as they met together. Just as life comes forth from the intimate relationship between husband and wife, so life comes forth from our intimate koinonia with Him.

Make a Distinction

Sadly, in most traditional church settings we don't draw a distinction between the body and blood of Jesus. We lump the bread and the cup all together and take communion only acknowledging the forgiveness of sin. When we take holy communion, we hold two elements in our hands, the bread and the cup. The bread represents the body of Jesus, and the cup represents His blood.

These are two distinct elements representing two distinct works and we should always recognize and honor them in their uniqueness.

The body of Jesus, represented in the bread, represents everything we need, even in the moment, to include our healing, our wholeness, our provision, our protection and our complete peace and welfare. The blood of Jesus, signified in the cup, represents the forgiveness of our sins and our righteousness, right standing with God.

Thus, this forgiveness and righteousness distinctly qualifies us to receive everything we need from the His broken body. The two elements go together, while representing two distinct works.

> *The two elements go together, while representing two distinct works.*

Thanksgiving Brings Sozo

Another word given for holy communion, or the Lord's Supper, is eucharist. Eucharist is defined as "thanksgiving." Let's look at a story that shows how thanksgiving brought sozo into the life of a leper. In Luke 17:11-19 we read:

Now on his way to Jerusalem, Jesus traveled along the border between Samaria and Galilee. As he was going into a village, ten men who had leprosy met him. They stood at a distance and called out in a loud voice, "Jesus,

Master, have pity on us!" When he saw them, he said, "Go, show yourselves to the priests." And as they went, they were cleansed.

One of them, when he saw he was healed, came back, praising God in a loud voice. He threw himself at Jesus' feet and thanked him—and he was a Samaritan. Jesus asked, "Were not all ten cleansed? Where are the other nine? Has no one returned to give praise to God except this foreigner?" Then he said to him, "Rise and go; your faith has made you well" (NIV).

In the King James Version, the word "well" in verse 19 is the word "whole" and the word "whole" is the Greek word sozo.

This one out of the ten who came back to thank Jesus also received sozo for anything else he needed in his life When we receive holy communion with a heart of gratitude and thanksgiving for what Jesus has done for us, it brings more sozo into our lives too.

Chapter Ten Study Guide Questions

Chapter 10 lists names in which God is called and identified in scripture. Of those names, write down the ones that stand out to you the most based on your life experiences.

_____

_____

Prior to reading this chapter, how did you view communion?

_____

_____

How will you receive communion differently moving forward?

_____

_____

Chapter Eleven:
Your Sozo Story

Most likely as you've been reading this book your mind has taken you back to times and places when you have experienced sozo in your life. Have you ever been saved from your sin, healed of some sickness or condition, delivered, or set free from something? Have you been preserved? (If you're still breathing then that answer is yes.) Have you known God's protection from some harmful or dangerous situation? Has God provided for you? And has He brought wholeness to any area of your life? If the answer to any of these questions is yes, then you've already experienced sozo in your life. You just may not have known there's a word that encompasses the things God has done in your life through the finished work of Jesus.

Sozo

Saved – Healed – Delivered – Preserved – Protected
Made Prosperous – Made Whole

You may now also recognize areas in your life that still need sozo, and with this fresh and new discovery of what God's included in your salvation package, you're ready, by faith, to receive sozo in these areas as well.

You'll never deserve sozo on your own, and you can't make it happen on your own. This gift of sozo must be received by faith. Paul wrote in Ephesians 2:8-9,

> *This gift of sozo must be received by faith.*

"For by grace you have been saved [sozo] through faith, and that not of yourselves; it is the gift of God, not of works, lest anyone should boast. Look at this same verse in the Amplified Bible: "For it is by grace [God's remarkable compassion and favor drawing you to Christ] that you have been saved [sozo] [actually delivered from judgment and given eternal life] through faith. And this [salvation] is not of yourselves [not through your own effort], but it is the [undeserved, gracious] gift of God; not as a result of [your] works [nor your attempts to keep the Law], so that no one will [be able to] boast or take credit in any way [for his salvation]."

Go Tell

If you've experienced sozo in any area of your life, then someone else needs to hear about it. A pastor and mentor of mine, Greg Kennedy, would often say, "Your experience and encounter with God may be personal, but it should never be private." And there's so much truth to that. If every God encounter was kept private, then no one would ever hear the Good News.

Your testimony is your personal account, or story, of what God has done for you, and someone needs to hear it. As God does something specific in your life, then you are specifically qualified to share that story with someone else.

> *Your testimony is your personal account, or story, of what God has done for you, and someone needs to hear it.*

Paul said it this way in 2 Corinthians 1:3-4: "Blessed [gratefully praised and adored] be the God and Father of our Lord Jesus Christ, the Father of mercies and the God of all comfort, who comforts and encourages us in every trouble so that we will be able to comfort and encourage those who are in any kind of trouble, with the comfort with which we ourselves are comforted by God."

The word "trouble" in this verse is the Greek word thlipsis and includes "affliction, burden, trouble, or persecution." As God brings sozo into your life you're then uniquely qualified to be used by God to share that with someone, especially someone whose need or needs may be the same, or similar to yours.

Spirit-Led, Lifestyle Evangelism

The best way I've found to share sozo with others is through what I call "Spirit-led, lifestyle evangelism." Now if that leaves you scratching your head, let me explain.

The way personal one-on-one evangelism was modeled for me growing up in church went something like this.

We would approach someone and ask, "Do you know if you're going to heaven or hell when you die?" I actually remember doing this on the playground. On the occasional evangelism training we would role-play this with one another. If the Q and A went according to plan, then we felt like it worked out great.

Starting with the above question, if the person responded by saying they weren't sure where they would go when they died, we would then explain more. Our next step was to convince them that they were a sinner and to try to get them to pray the "sinner's prayer" with us. If they did so, then we were stoked!

Occasionally on a Saturday morning, a group of men and young guys, of which I was usually the youngest, would meet at the church to go out "soul winning." We would form up in pairs and head out to talk to people. When we later met back at the church, those who had gotten someone to pray the sinner's prayer were celebrated. The problem was that most all the people who prayed that prayer never showed up to church themselves. They never followed the Lord in believer's baptism and were never discipled. Yet we kept them on our score card for "souls we had won to Christ" for that year.

Please don't get me wrong. I'm not poking fun at, or mocking, this form of evangelism. My grandfather came to Christ that very way. Some men from Calvary Baptist Church in Greenville, North Carolina, knocked on his door one day and Edward Mumford prayed the sinner's prayer and he really meant it.

From that day on his life was never the same. He and his wife, Larue, would load up their five kids in the bread truck, his work vehicle and the only vehicle that would fit the whole family, and head to church. Sunday morning, Sunday night, and Wednesday night they faithfully attended and were discipled.

As Ed drove around eastern North Carolina delivering bread to stores, his bread route became his evangelism field. That "soul-winning knock" on his door really changed my grandfather's life that day, for which I will be forever grateful. But it still begs the question, are there other ways to reach the lost?

The Samaritan woman Jesus met at the well is a perfect picture of Spirit-led, lifestyle evangelism. Her encounter with Jesus led to her being made whole in an area she never thought possible. She received sozo for herself, and then she supernaturally went into town telling others what Jesus had done for her. It wasn't an evangelism formula for her.

We know that going out into town talking to people about her life was a supernatural event for her, because in the natural she didn't want to be around the town folk. That's why she would come out to the well in the heat of the day to draw water. She was ashamed and felt condemned because of where her life was. But when she found the sozo that only Jesus could give her, she supernaturally went out to tell others. Her sozo story made such an impact that the whole town went to see Jesus for themselves and begged Him not to leave. Jesus stayed and taught them for two more days, revealing to them all that He was indeed the Messiah, and many put their faith and trust in Him.

> *But when she found the sozo that only Jesus could give her, she supernaturally went out to tell others*

The demoniac man who encountered Jesus, and whose life was changed, went out to ten cities throughout the region supernaturally sharing his sozo story. There are many examples of people in the New Testament who received sozo for themselves and then supernaturally shared it with others.

Spirit-led, lifestyle evangelism takes all the pressure off you. Our focus is to simply receive by grace, through faith, what God has done for us through Jesus. Then, we

> *Spirit-led, lifestyle evangelism takes all the pressure off you.*

can pray asking the Lord to use us, through the power of the Holy Spirit, to share the Good News of Jesus with others. You'll be amazed at how well this works! You'll simply be minding your own business one day and find yourself in conversation with someone. And without even thinking about it, you'll have shared your sozo story and the Good News of Jesus with another. Later it will dawn on you that God answered your prayer! He used you, just as you had asked Him, in a supernatural way. I've personally experienced this way of evangelizing many times, to the glory of God. We allow Him to touch our lives with sozo, and with the help and leading of the Holy Spirit we share with others. Today, receive what you need, then let the Holy Spirit work through you to share.

Be a Link

In 1 Corinthians 3:5-9 Paul described what I call the "evangelism chain." He said in essence that some plant, or sew, some water, but God gives the increase. You may be the one who plants the sozo seed, waters the sozo seed, or you could be the one God uses to harvest the sozo seed. What matters is that you are simply a chain in the link.

Bruce Thigpen, from Dublin, Georgia, was a Marine I served with many years ago. Bruce was such an awesome guy and the epitome of a young "southern gentleman." We went through boot camp together, completed job-training school together, and were stationed together at Camp Lejeune, North Carolina, where we were roommates.

Bruce grew up going to church like I did, and though he wasn't overtly religious, Bruce was indeed a believer. One day a new guy moved in with us. Matt was from upstate New York and a super great guy as well. Bruce and I both liked Matt a lot and one day the topic of God came up. Matt, in a polite, but direct way let Bruce and I both know that he didn't want anything to do with God.

In fact, the way he said it led Bruce and me to believe that Matt was an atheist or agnostic. As two southern boys who had grown up in the Bible Belt, we were beside ourselves at the thought of having an atheist living in our room. These Marine Corps barracks rooms weren't that big, and we were afraid that a lightning strike sent down from Heaven might take us all out!

We didn't push Matt, but occasionally something we said watered the seed as God shined His light through us. I say "watered" because the truth was that the seed of salvation had been sewn in Matt way earlier, but he just wasn't ready.

After Camp Lejeune I lost contact with Matt, but one day out of nowhere, over twenty years later, he sent me a Facebook message. He reached out to say that he and his wife were on vacation at the North Carolina coast and were planning on attending the church I was pastoring that following Sunday. We had a great time catching up! It was great seeing Matt again after all those years! And I was surprised when Matt told me he had been following me on social media for years and often watched and listened to my sermons.

Matt shared that somewhere along the way he had accepted Jesus Christ, and I can't even begin to tell you what that did for my heart!

You don't have to hit the evangelism game-winning grand slam, although on occasion you might just do that. But just being willing to get a runner on base, by planting or watering, can be enough. If we're faithful and willing to do that part, with the help of the Holy Spirit, then we can leave it up to God to bring them home.

> *If we're faithful and willing to do that part, with the help of the Holy Spirit, then we can leave it up to God to bring them home.*

Let It Shine

My youngest child, age two and a half, just learned the song "This Little Light of Mine." As he walks around singing it, in his little precious voice, my wife Jen and I get big smiles on our faces.

I'm pretty sure there's nothing that puts a smile on the Father's face more than when we let our light shine. Paul called it "the light of the gospel of the glory of Christ" (2 Corinthians 4:4). We let His light in, then He shines it through us to others.

My friend Rick shared a story with me about a cafeteria worker who let her light shine and that light reached his brother-in-law. John married Rick's older sister when Rick was just ten years old. Rick looked up to John, but John was not a good role model for Rick at all. As you might say, John was "rough as a cob" and drank too much, smoked too much, often got high and had a foul mouth.

As Rick got older, he had a huge burden in his heart for John, but every time he tried to talk to John about the Lord, John didn't want to hear it. John wanted nothing to do with God and emphatically told Rick he didn't want to talk to him about "his Jesus." John knew he was a sinner and he wanted to stay that way.

The years of rough living finally caught up with him, and at sixty-five John found himself in a hospital dying of COPD and emphysema. Everyone knew John didn't have long to live, and Rick couldn't bear the thought of John dying without Jesus. Rick went to visit him in the hospital to make one final attempt at reaching John, but even in his hospital bed John told Rick that he still didn't want to hear anything about God. John flat out rejected Jesus and Rick's heart was breaking.

The next morning, however, Rick was shocked to get a text from John asking Rick to come to the hospital as soon as he could. John had something amazing he wanted to tell Rick.

As rough of a guy as John was, there was at least one good thing you could say about him—John loved his wife, RoxAnn! John and RoxAnn's love for each other is the only thing that had managed to keep them together through the years.

That day was RoxAnn's birthday, and John was hurting on the inside because he couldn't do something special for his wife to celebrate. As John was lying there helpless, feeling down, and discouraged, he heard a knock at the door. A cafeteria worker named Barb came in and introduced herself to John and wanted to talk with him about meal options for the next few days. Somewhere in the conversation John told Barb that it was his wife's birthday, and she responded by telling him that she would have a special meal delivered that night for their dinner to celebrate.

The thought of that put a huge smile on John's face, and as Barb was leaving, she asked, "Can I pray with you?" John said yes, and Barb took his hand to pray. At that moment Barb's light became electric! As John told Rick, when she began to pray with him, he felt the power of God go through his whole body. With tears rolling down his face, as she prayed for him, John threw both of his hands in the air toward Heaven and said, "Lord, please forgive me of all my sins, and please take care of my wife and family." With that,

At that moment Barb's light became electric!

John received Jesus Christ into his life as his Lord and Savior!

I can hear my little son Jonas singing it now:
Let it shine! Let it shine! Let it shine!
Jesus is the Light!
I'm gonna let it shine!
Jesus is the Light!
I'm gonna it shine!
Jesus is the Light!
I'm gonna let it shine!
Let it shine! Let it shine! Let it shine!
Will you let the glorious light of the sozo gospel shine in your life, then through you to others? Somebody, just like John, needs your light today!

Chapter Eleven Study Guide Questions

List areas in which you have received sozo in your life.

_____

_____

List some moments in which you shared your sozo story with another.

_____

_____

Does the concept of "Spirit-led, lifestyle evangelism" change or enhance the way you see evangelism? If so, explain.

_____

_____

Is there one or more people in your life that you are believing God for their salvation? If so, list their names below and take a moment to pray for them.

_____

_____

Chapter Twelve:
Take Your Seat

In the Old Testament we see the story of David and Jonathan. Although they should have been enemies, they loved each other dearly. Jonathan was King Saul's son and Saul wanted David dead. But David and Jonathan made a covenant and promise together that they would always do good to each other and their families as well. Long after Jonathan had died in battle and David had been on the throne as king, David remembered this covenant that he had made with Jonathan. In 2 Samuel 9:1, David asked, "Is there anyone still left of the house of Saul to whom I can show kindness for Jonathan's sake?" (NIV).

David learned that Mephibosheth was the only child of Jonathan still alive. Mephibosheth, now grown and crippled from a fall when he was dropped as a child, lived in a place called Lo Debar.

David sent for Mephibosheth to come to the palace. Mephibosheth was afraid, thinking David may want to kill him, but instead David restored to Mephibosheth everything that had belonged to his grandfather, King Saul. On top of that, David also made a permanent seat for Mephibosheth at the king's own royal table.

Mephibosheth would never again have to worry about how he was going to survive. His life went from dark and dreary to sunny days ahead! In an instant he was "fully supplied in need or want of nothing!" And with a permanent seat at the king's table, Mephibosheth would never go hungry but enjoy only the best and as much as he wanted.

It's interesting to note that the place in which Mephibosheth had lived for so long, Lo Debar, in Hebrew means "no word."

Sadly, many God-loving Christians have never heard the word that Jesus died not only so that we may go to heaven, but also so that we may have and enjoy abundant life here on this earth. I'm not saying that we'll never go through challenges or

> *Jesus died not only so that we may go to heaven, but also so that we may have and enjoy abundant life here on this earth.*

trying times. Jesus made that clear in John 16:33: "In this world you will have trouble. But take heart!

I have overcome the world" (NIV). Notice the second part of that verse? He has overcome the world for us! Because Jesus has overcome the world for us, even when we go through trying times and seasons, we can do so with a hope and expectation that things will always get better.

Today you and I are beneficiaries of a New Covenant with God through Jesus Christ. This New Covenant is far superior to any Old Testament Covenant, because this covenant has been ratified through the blood of Jesus. As we close, let's look at a few verses about this New Covenant.

After supper he took another cup of wine and said, "This cup is the new covenant between God and his people — an agreement confirmed with my blood, which is poured out as a sacrifice for you." (Luke 22:20 NLT)

In the same way also he took the cup, after supper, saying, "This cup is the new covenant in my blood. Do this, as often as you drink it, in remembrance of me." (1 Corinthians 11:25 CSB)

But now Jesus, our High Priest, has been given a ministry that is far superior to the old priesthood, for he is the one who mediates for us a far better covenant with God, based on better promises. (Hebrew 8:6)

That is why he is the one who mediates a new covenant between God and people, so that all who are called can receive the eternal inheritance God has promised them. For Christ died to set them free from the penalty of the sins they had committed under that first covenant. (Hebrews 9:15)

Because of this New Covenant you and I have a permanent seat at the table! From this day forward, with the Lord's help, may we never live another day in Lo Debar again!

My Prayer for You

Father, I pray that the words You've given me to write down in this book, You would use to make an eternal difference in the life of this reader. I pray, Father, that through the power of Your Spirit You would make known to them the richness of the inheritance we have been given through Christ. I pray that You would show and demonstrate sozo salvation in every area of their life and that they would allow Your Spirit to work through them to share this Light with others. I pray this in the powerful name of Jesus! Amen!!!

Chapter Twelve Study Guide Questions

Like Mephibosheth, have you found yourself living in a place of "no word" when it comes to all that Jesus Christ has provided for you through His finished work on the cross? If so, share some thoughts below.

_____
_____

Considering the truth of sozo, in what areas will you take your seat at the table of the abundant life Jesus has provided for you?

_____
_____

What are your three biggest takeaways from what has been shared in this book?

_____
_____

Acknowledgments

I am so grateful for those who have contributed to this book. Without their help this would not have been possible. I would like to thank my wife, Jen, for working so tirelessly to make every detail as excellent as possible. I also want to thank Kevin Harvey of Harvey Books Editorial Services who I'm sure had no idea what he was in for! A huge thank you to Bryce Mallette, Jared Mosley and Mike Sharpe for contributing to the study guide questions and thank you also to Mike for helping publish the book. Also, to my six wonderful children, Brittany and Chris, Joel, Courtney, Faith and Jonas who inspire me and pray for me. And, for the many friends and family who bathed this book in prayer, thank you. Lastly and most importantly, I simply want to thank my heavenly Father for pouring the sozo revelation into my heart and for giving me the honor and privilege of telling His story.

Step-By-Step Instructions for using BlueLetterBible.org

In your browser, type in blueletterbible.org

In the search bar, type in the verse reference you would like to look up, like John 3:17, and hit the "Go" tab.

Click the verse reference you want to search. It is highlighted in blue.

Scroll down and find the specific word you want to look up.

Note: The word you are searching will be seen on the left and its equivalent Greek word will appear in the column on the right.

Click on the Strong's reference number for the word you are searching. This is highlighted in blue and is in the middle column. For example, the reference for "saved" is Strong's G4982.

As you scroll down you will see all the definitions related to the word you are searching within the section "Outline of Biblical Usage."

Made in the USA
Middletown, DE
28 May 2022